YOU CAN DRAW IT!

BIRDS OF PREY

ILLUSTRATED BY STEVE PORTER

BELLWETHER MEDIA · MINNEAPOLIS, MN

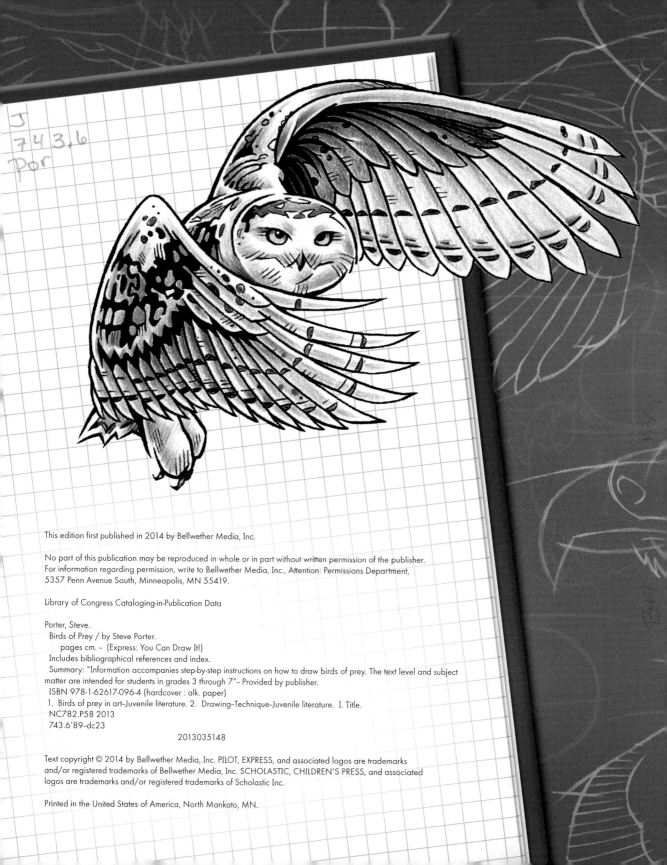

This edition first published in 2014 by Bellwether Media, Inc.

No part of this publication may be reproduced in whole or in part without written permission of the publisher.
For information regarding permission, write to Bellwether Media, Inc., Attention: Permissions Department,
5357 Penn Avenue South, Minneapolis, MN 55419.

Library of Congress Cataloging-in-Publication Data

Porter, Steve.
  Birds of Prey / by Steve Porter.
      pages cm. – (Express: You Can Draw It!)
  Includes bibliographical references and index.
  Summary: "Information accompanies step-by-step instructions on how to draw birds of prey. The text level and subject
matter are intended for students in grades 3 through 7"– Provided by publisher.
  ISBN 978-1-62617-096-4 (hardcover : alk. paper)
  1. Birds of prey in art–Juvenile literature. 2. Drawing–Technique–Juvenile literature. I. Title.
  NC782.P58 2013
  743.6'89–dc23
                            2013035148

Printed in the United States of America, North Mankato, MN.

TABLE OF CONTENTS

BIRDS OF PREY!

Birds of prey are majestic animals known for their strength and beauty. They use their sharp sense of sight to hunt for their dinner from high up in the air. Some are powerful **predators**. They take down animals that are too big for most birds to handle. Others are **scavengers** that look for dead animals to feast on. No matter their meal choice, all **raptors** use strong **talons** and sharp beaks to tear apart their food.

DRAWING FROM PHOTOS IS A GREAT PLACE TO START. WORK YOUR WAY UP TO DRAWING FROM MEMORY OR YOUR IMAGINATION.

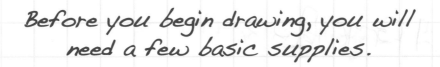

Before you begin drawing, you will need a few basic supplies.

PAPER

DRAWING
PENCILS

2B OR NOT 2B?

NOT ALL DRAWING PENCILS ARE
THE SAME. "B" PENCILS ARE
SOFTER, MAKE DARKER MARKS,
AND SMUDGE EASILY. "H" PENCILS
ARE HARDER, MAKE LIGHTER
MARKS, AND DON'T SMUDGE
VERY MUCH AT ALL.

BLACK INK
PEN

COLORED PENCILS
(ALL DRAWINGS IN THIS BOOK WERE
FINISHED WITH COLORED PENCILS.)

ERASER

PENCIL
SHARPENER

Bald Eagle
The Patriotic Bird

Bald eagles are not actually bald. They get their name from the white feathers that crown their heads. The sight of a bald eagle soaring through the sky is an impressive one. That is why the bird is an important symbol. Native Americans use the bald eagle as an image of strength and courage. For the United States, the bald eagle is the national bird. It represents the American spirit of freedom.

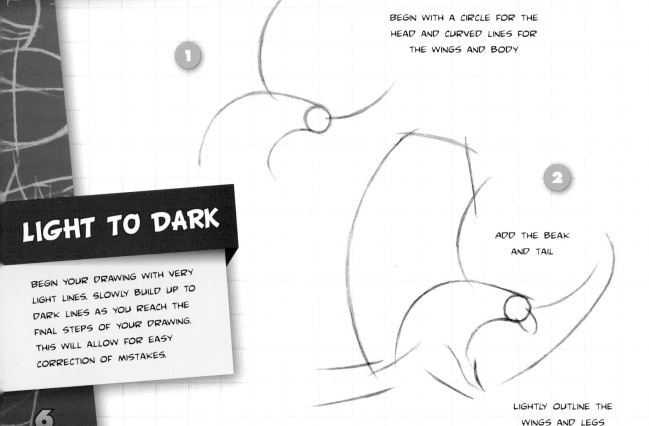

1

BEGIN WITH A CIRCLE FOR THE HEAD AND CURVED LINES FOR THE WINGS AND BODY

2

ADD THE BEAK AND TAIL

LIGHTLY OUTLINE THE WINGS AND LEGS

LIGHT TO DARK

BEGIN YOUR DRAWING WITH VERY LIGHT LINES. SLOWLY BUILD UP TO DARK LINES AS YOU REACH THE FINAL STEPS OF YOUR DRAWING. THIS WILL ALLOW FOR EASY CORRECTION OF MISTAKES.

ADD FEATHER DETAILS
TO THE WINGS, BODY,
AND TAIL

3

ADD THE EYES
AND TALONS

4

ADD SHADING
DETAIL TO
THE BIRD

5

INK AND COLOR

BALD EAGLES ARE DARK BROWN WITH
WHITE HEADS AND TAILS. THEIR BEAKS
AND TALONS ARE BRIGHT YELLOW.

7

Peregrine Falcon
The Fastest Flier

Peregrine falcons are the fastest birds in the world. They can reach speeds of 200 miles (320 kilometers) per hour! They need their speed for hunting smaller birds. First, they fly up to 3,000 feet (915 meters) above their prey. When it is time to attack, they tuck their wings and go into a high-speed dive called a **stoop**.

1

START WITH TWO OVALS
FOR THE HEAD AND BODY

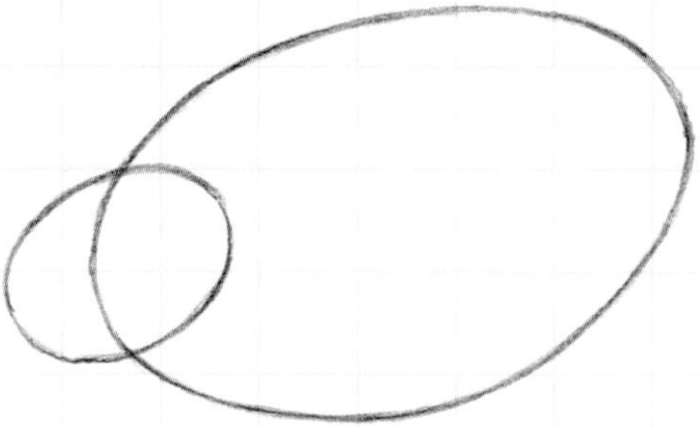

2

ADD THE EYES
AND BEAK

SKETCH THE
OUTLINE OF THE
WINGS AND TAIL

3

ADD DETAILS TO THE
HEAD AND NECK

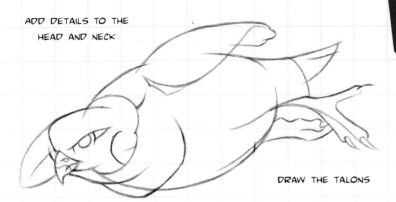

JUST A HINT

IT'S NOT NECESSARY TO INCLUDE EVERY
FEATHER AND SPOT ON YOUR SUBJECT.
A FEW SCATTERED DETAILS CAN GIVE THE
EFFECT. YOU CAN FINISH YOUR DRAWING A
LITTLE FASTER THIS WAY.

DRAW THE TALONS

4

ADD SHADING TO
THE EYE, FEATHERS,
AND TALONS

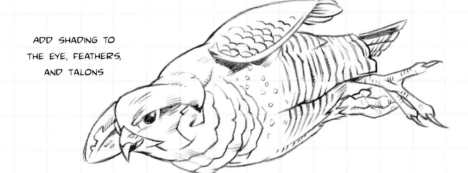

INK AND COLOR

5

PEREGRINE FALCONS ARE
BLUISH GRAY AND WHITE ON
TOP. THEIR UNDERSIDES ARE
CREAM WITH BLACK.

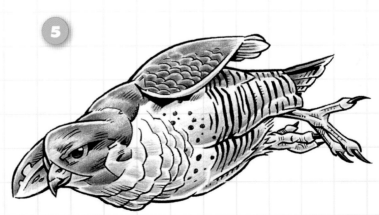

Red-tailed Hawk
The Screeching Bird

Red-tailed hawks are named for their dark orange-red tails. These colorful tails make it easy to spot them flying circles in the air. However, red-tailed hawks are possibly more famous for their **shrill** screams. Their screeches warn other raptors to stay out of their territories. Red-tailed hawks commonly make it into movies and television programs for being loudmouths.

1

BEGIN WITH TWO
OVALS FOR THE HEAD
AND BODY

SEE THE BIG PICTURE

WAIT TO ADD DETAILS UNTIL YOU ARE HAPPY WITH THE BASIC SHAPE OF YOUR DRAWING. YOU DON'T WANT TO SPEND TIME DETAILING A PART OF YOUR DRAWING THAT WILL BE ERASED LATER.

ADD THE EYE

2

ADD LINES FOR THE
WINGS, BEAK, LEGS,
AND TAIL

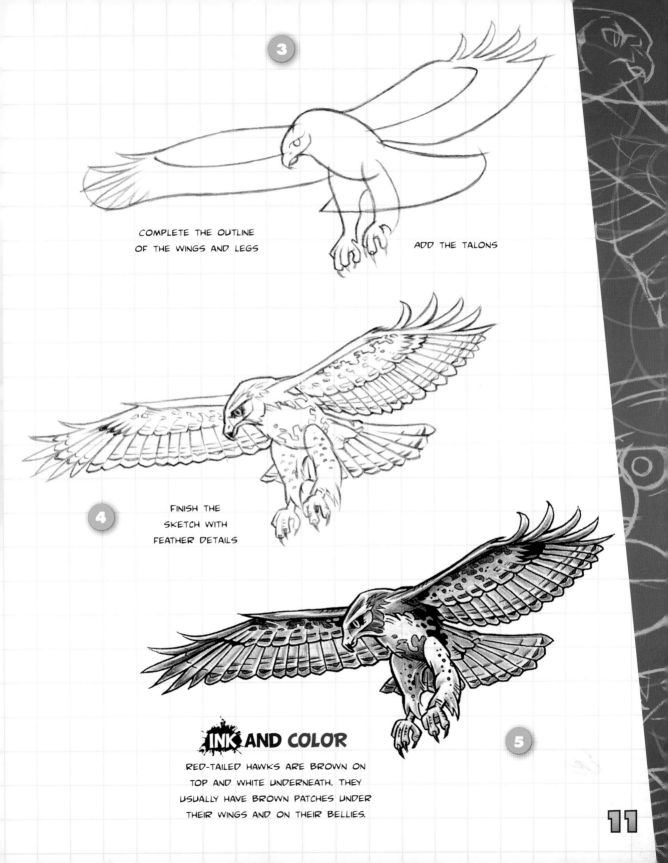

3

COMPLETE THE OUTLINE
OF THE WINGS AND LEGS

ADD THE TALONS

4

FINISH THE
SKETCH WITH
FEATHER DETAILS

INK AND COLOR

5

RED-TAILED HAWKS ARE BROWN ON
TOP AND WHITE UNDERNEATH. THEY
USUALLY HAVE BROWN PATCHES UNDER
THEIR WINGS AND ON THEIR BELLIES.

Eurasian Eagle Owl

The Adaptable Owl

Eurasian eagle owls have bright orange eyes and fluffy **ear tufts**. They like to live on rocky cliffs, but many can also be found in forests and near deserts. Eagle owls are **adaptable** because they are not picky eaters. They will hunt almost any animal they see, small or large. Eagle owls can overpower big prey with their 6.5-foot (2-meter) wingspan!

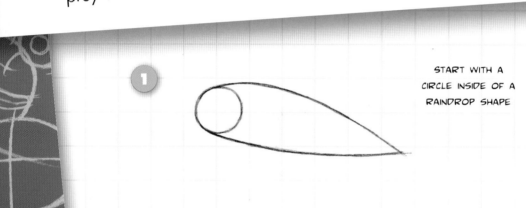

1

START WITH A
CIRCLE INSIDE OF A
RAINDROP SHAPE

ADD THE EYE
AND BEAK

USE YOUR ARM

DRAW WITH YOUR WHOLE ARM, NOT
JUST YOUR WRIST AND FINGERS.

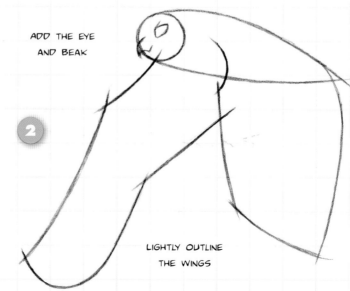

2

LIGHTLY OUTLINE
THE WINGS

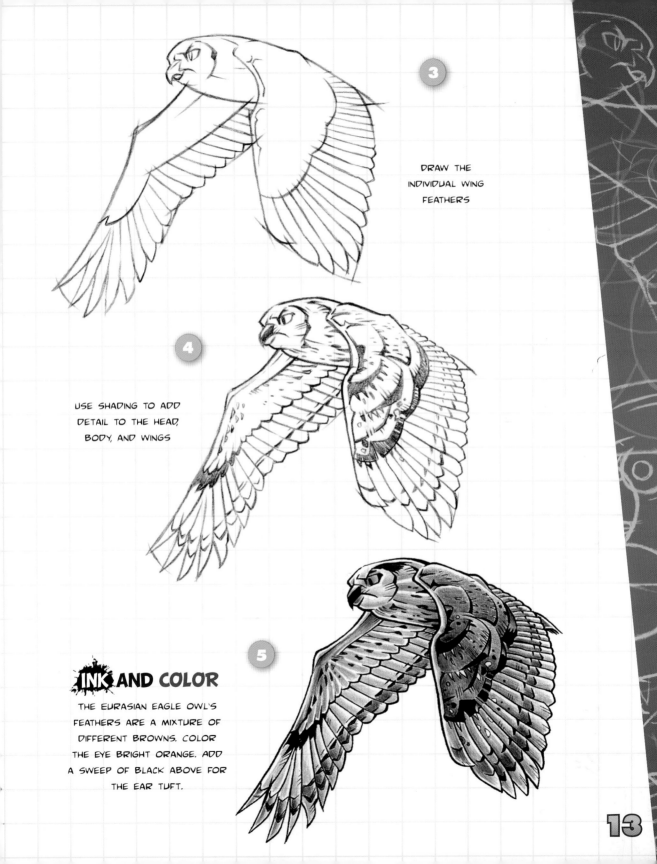

3

DRAW THE
INDIVIDUAL WING
FEATHERS

4

USE SHADING TO ADD
DETAIL TO THE HEAD,
BODY, AND WINGS

5

INK AND COLOR

THE EURASIAN EAGLE OWL'S
FEATHERS ARE A MIXTURE OF
DIFFERENT BROWNS. COLOR
THE EYE BRIGHT ORANGE. ADD
A SWEEP OF BLACK ABOVE FOR
THE EAR TUFT.

Golden Eagle
The Sport Hunter

Golden eagles live in the open countryside. Here, the hunting is good. They can snatch small prey such as rabbits, squirrels, and prairie dogs. When these animals are not available, golden eagles make large animals their dinner. They have been seen hunting full-grown deer! They catch these big animals with dives as fast as 150 miles (241 kilometers) per hour!

BREAK IT DOWN

JUST ABOUT ANY SUBJECT CAN BE BROKEN INTO SMALLER PARTS. LOOK FOR CIRCLES, OVALS, SQUARES, AND OTHER BASIC SHAPES THAT CAN HELP BUILD YOUR DRAWING.

1

START WITH A CURVED LINE COMING OUT OF AN OVAL

2

ADD THE EYE AND CURVED LINES FOR THE NECK

COMPLETE THE OUTLINE OF THE BEAK

3

ADD DETAILS TO THE
AREA AROUND THE EYE

BEGIN TO
ADD FEATHERS

4

ADD MORE FEATHERS

SHADE TO ADD
FINISHING DETAILS

5

INK AND COLOR

GOLDEN EAGLES HAVE BROWN
FEATHERS ON THEIR HEADS.
THEIR YELLOW BEAKS HAVE
BLACK TIPS.

15

Snowy Owl
The Frosty Flier

Snowy owls are usually found in cold areas, so they have thick feathers for **insulation**. These feathers make them the heaviest owls in North America! Snowy owls like to hunt in wide-open fields. They use their catlike yellow eyes to spot mice, rabbits, and small birds. Their white feathers help them sneak up on prey in their wintry surroundings.

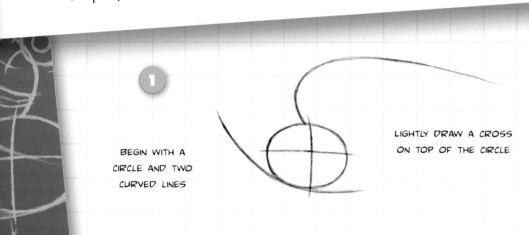

1

BEGIN WITH A
CIRCLE AND TWO
CURVED LINES

LIGHTLY DRAW A CROSS
ON TOP OF THE CIRCLE

JUST WALK AWAY

IF YOU'RE STUCK ON A CERTAIN PART
OF YOUR DRAWING, IT IS SOMETIMES
BEST TO WALK AWAY. COME BACK
LATER WITH A FRESH APPROACH.

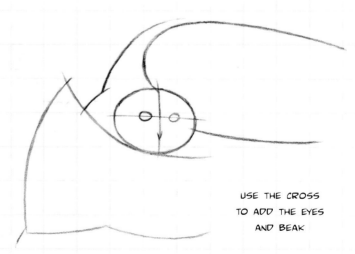

2

ADD LINES FOR
THE WINGS

USE THE CROSS
TO ADD THE EYES
AND BEAK

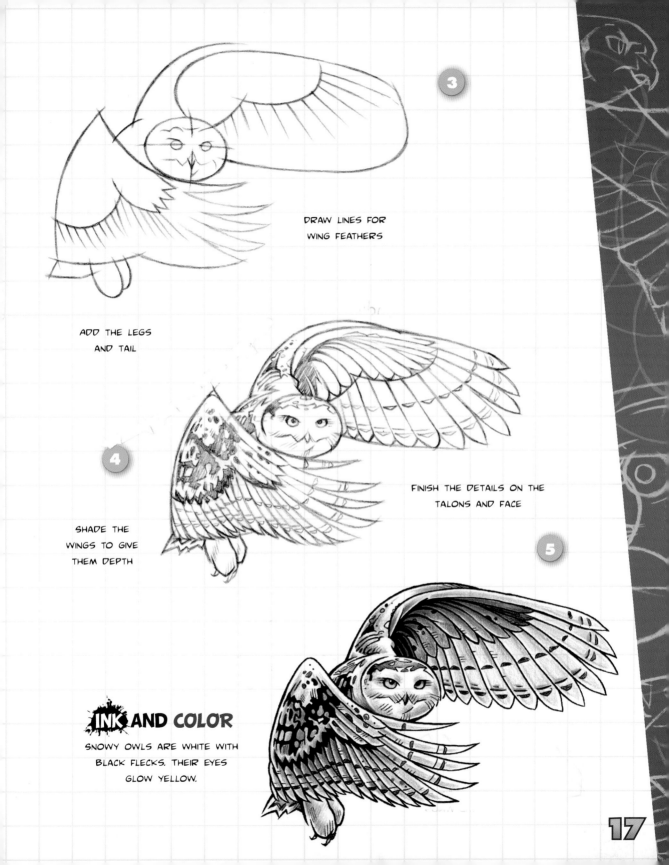

DRAW LINES FOR
WING FEATHERS

③

ADD THE LEGS
AND TAIL

④

FINISH THE DETAILS ON THE
TALONS AND FACE

SHADE THE
WINGS TO GIVE
THEM DEPTH

⑤

INK AND COLOR

SNOWY OWLS ARE WHITE WITH
BLACK FLECKS. THEIR EYES
GLOW YELLOW.

17

Harpy Eagle
The Legendary Hunter

Harpy eagles are the most powerful raptors in North and South America. They fly through the **rain forest** in search of large prey such as monkeys and sloths. These patient birds will wait on a perch for up to 23 hours to spot a meal. From a distance, they can see even a slight movement through the **canopy**.

1

DRAW TWO OVALS
CONNECTED BY A LINE

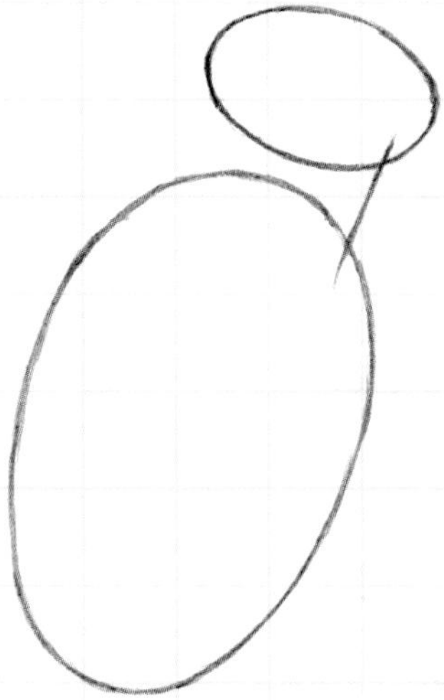

BEGIN THE EYE, BEAK, HEAD
FEATHERS, AND WINGS

2

ADD LINES FOR
THE LEGS, PERCH,
AND TAIL

3

DRAW INDIVIDUAL
FEATHERS AND COMPLETE
THE TAIL OUTLINE

4

USE SHADING
AND LITTLE LINES
TO ADD FINISHING
DETAILS

ADD THE TALONS
AND THE REST OF
THE PERCH

TESTING, 1...2...3!

BEFORE YOU ADD COLOR TO
YOUR DRAWING, TEST SOME
COLORS OR COMBINATIONS OF
COLORS ON THE SIDE TO FIND
THE PERFECT SHADE.

5

INK AND COLOR

HARPY EAGLES ARE DARK GRAY
WITH WHITE BELLIES. BLACK
FEATHERS ACCENT THEIR BODIES.

19

California Condor
The Soaring Bird

California condors are the largest birds that fly in North America. Their wings measure almost 10 feet (3 meters) wide! California condors can soar up to 15,000 feet (4,572 meters) high. These excellent gliders barely flap their huge wings. Instead, they use **wind currents** to **propel** themselves upward.

1

BEGIN WITH A LITTLE CIRCLE AND A LARGE OVAL

2

ADD THE TAIL AND LINES TO START THE WINGS AND LEGS

STAY BACK

HOLD YOUR PENCIL A LITTLE FARTHER BACK FROM THE TIP. THIS ALLOWS YOU TO DRAW LONGER, SMOOTHER LINES.

3 FINISH THE OUTLINE
OF THE WINGS

DRAW THE TALONS
AND FACIAL DETAILS

4 SKETCH INDIVIDUAL FEATHERS

USE SHADING TO
ADD MORE DETAIL
TO THE FEATHERS

5

INK AND COLOR

CALIFORNIA CONDORS ARE BLACK WITH WHITE
STREAKS UNDER THEIR WINGS. THEIR BALD
HEADS ARE PINK WITH SOME PURPLE.

GLOSSARY

adaptable—able to change to fit in different environments and situations

canopy—the covering of leafy branches formed by the tops of the trees

ear tufts—long feathers above the eyes of some birds

insulation—protection that traps heat

predators—animals that hunt other animals for food

propel—to push in a specific direction

rain forest—a thick, green forest that receives a lot of rainfall

raptors—birds that have good vision, strong talons, and sharp beaks to hunt

scavengers—animals that feed on the remains of dead animals

shrill—a high-pitched shriek

stoop—a high-speed dive

talons—long, sharp claws on the feet of birds of prey

wind currents—the movement of air due to differences in pressure

TO LEARN MORE

At the Library

De la Bedoyere, Camilla. *100 Things You Should Know About Birds of Prey.* Broomall, Pa.: Mason Crest Pub., 2011.

Green, John. *How to Draw Birds.* Mineola, N.Y.: Dover Publications, 2009.

Laubach, Christyna M. *Raptor! A Kid's Guide to Birds of Prey.* North Adams, Mass.: Storey Books, 2002.

On the Web

Learning more about birds of prey is as easy as 1, 2, 3.

1. Go to www.factsurfer.com.

2. Enter "birds of prey" into the search box.

3. Click the "Surf" button and you will see a list of related Web sites.

With factsurfer.com, finding more information is just a click away.

INDEX